EXPLORING THE SCIENCE OF NATURE

The Nature and Science of
FLOWERS

Jane Burton and Kim Taylor

Gareth Stevens Publishing
MILWAUKEE

For a free color catalog describing Gareth Stevens Publishing's list of high-quality books
and multimedia programs, call 1-800-542-2595 (USA) or 1-800-461-9120 (Canada).
Gareth Stevens Publishing's Fax: (414) 225-0377.
See our catalog, too, on the World Wide Web: gsinc.com

Library of Congress Cataloging-in-Publication Data

Burton, Jane.
The nature and science of flowers / by Jane Burton and Kim Taylor.
p. cm. -- (Exploring the science of nature)
Includes bibliographical references and index.
Summary: Explains the purpose and parts of flowers, how they make seeds,
and how their color, freshness, and scent give pleasure to both people and animals.
ISBN 0-8368-2106-8 (lib. bdg.)
1. Flowers—Juvenile literature. [1. Flowers.] I. Taylor, Kim. II. Title.
III. Series: Burton, Jane. Exploring the science of nature.
QK653.B948   1998
582.13—dc21   97-53119

First published in North America in 1998 by
Gareth Stevens Publishing
1555 North RiverCenter Drive, Suite 201
Milwaukee, Wisconsin 53212 USA

Contents

Words that appear in the glossary are printed in **boldface** type the first time they occur in the text.

Why Plants Have Flowers

Flowers display a wonderful variety of colors — delicate pink, sky blue, rich crimson, and the purest yellows and whites. The colors, scents, and freshness of flowers give pleasure to people throughout the world. We enjoy their beauty, even though we know they will not last. Of course, plants do not grow flowers just for people. They grow them for their own special purpose.

Flowers allow the **genes** of plants to mix. This means that, instead of producing offspring that are all exactly alike, a flowering plant produces a variety of offspring, each slightly different from the next. These small differences are important because they would allow some plants to survive when others might die. If all plants were identical, they would all die if the climate changed and conditions became difficult.

Flowers produce male **cells in the form of fine** grains called **pollen**. Insects and certain other types of animals carry pollen to other flowers of the same **species**. The male cells from one flower join with female cells of another flower. This process, called **fertilization**, leads to the formation of seeds. Seeds carry different mixtures of genes.

Below: A meadow in North America with broad-leaved fireweed and purple daisies.

Below: Springtime in Australia with showy sunray, pink everlasting, and ciliate-fruited daisies.

Petals and Sepals

Top: An opening bud of mallow reveals a ring of protective green **sepals**.

Below: A trillium flower has three petals.

Below: Honesty has four petals.

Right: Each of the five petals of red campion has two lobes.

Right: The five petals of Mexican butter-wort are not all the same shape.

Petals are often the most noticeable parts of a flower. They are brightly colored, delicate structures that may last only a short time. The number of petals on a flower depends on the particular plant species. Three-, four-, five-, and six-petaled flowers are common. Above six, the number of petals may vary from flower to flower on the same plant. Certain types of flowers seem to have dozens of petals. Sunflowers, for instance, have a ring of multiple petals surrounding a central disk. But close inspection reveals that sunflowers actually are made up of many tiny flowers, called **florets**, joined together. Most of the florets have no petals at all, whereas those around the edge of the disk have one petal each. This is true of many other flowers in the daisy family. Other families of plants produce flowers in which the petals are joined to form a single trumpet-shaped tube.

Left: Each floret around the edge of an ox-eye daisy has one white petal. The florets in the central disk have no petals.

Below: Queen cup has six equal petals.

Sepals grow in a ring close behind the petals of many flowers. There are usually the same number of sepals as petals, but sepals are much tougher and are usually green. Sepals protect the petals before the flower opens.

Below: Bluebell petals join at their bases to form a tube but separate toward their tips.

Below: Morning glory petals join to form a trumpet-shaped tube.

Below: Menzies banksia flowers are so close together, there is no room for petals.

Stamens and Stigmas

Top: The **stigma** of a Christmas cactus flower projects beyond the stamens.

The main purpose of flowers is to produce seeds. Seed production takes place in the middle of the flower. There, **stamens** hold masses of bright yellow, orange, or even purple pollen at their tips. As the flower opens, the stamens lengthen, and the pollen becomes fluffy and ready to spill out.

The stigma is in the very middle of the flower, surrounded by the stamens. It often looks like a stamen without pollen, but it has a completely different purpose.

The stigma collects pollen from other flowers on its sticky tip. Some kinds of flowers may have several stigmas.

Right: The stamens of a tulip carry a mass of yellow pollen grains on their clubbed ends. The stigma, at the center of the flower, is ready to receive pollen from another tulip.

8

The stalk supporting the stigma (the **style**) runs down into the heart of the flower. Here, the female cells grow in a special swelling called the **ovary**. A pollen grain on the stigma starts to grow, sending a thin tube down inside the style.

Male genes from the grain travel down this tube to join with female genes in the ovary to form seeds. This is where fertilization and gene mixing take place.

Above: When rosebay first opens, its stigma is closed and folded back beneath the flower, out of the way of the forward-projecting stamens.

After the stamens shed their pollen, the style begins to straighten, and the stigma opens.

When the stigma is fully open and ready to receive pollen, the spent stamens fold back. These movements and their timing help prevent self-fertilization.

One House or Two?

Top: A hazel tree carries both male **catkins** and tiny red female flowers.

There is tremendous variety in the design of flowers, and not all flowers have both stamens and stigmas. Some plants produce male flowers separate from female flowers. In this way, there is no risk of pollen from the stamens of a flower getting onto its own stigma. This would result in self-fertilization and seeds with the same genes as their parent plant. Most plants try to avoid self-fertilization because it reduces variation.

In some species, the whole plant is either male or female. Plants with separate sexes are said to be **dioecious**. *Oecious* is from the Greek word *oikos*,

Right: A male goat willow tree carries catkins covered with yellow stamens. This tree cannot produce seeds.

meaning "house." For example, willow trees may be either male, with bright yellow pollen-covered catkins, or female, with green catkins.

Plants whose flowers carry both male and female parts are called **monoecious**. Everything that is necessary for producing seeds is contained within one "house." Many monoecious garden plants and weeds rely on self-fertilization. It is a sure way of producing seeds.

An even better method is to do away with fertilization altogether. That is exactly what dandelions and several other common plants have done. These plants are clones. All the plants in one area have identical genes. These plants may be in trouble if the climate changes and they are unable to change with it because of their lack of variation.

Above: Dandelions mainly produce seeds without fertilization. But they still produce pollen, even though it is not needed.

Left: A female goat willow tree has green catkins that carry many small stigmas. This tree will produce masses of fluffy white seeds in late summer.

11

Above: A honeybee collects **nectar** and pollen from hemlock water dropwort flowers. It stores the pollen grains in special sacs on its hind legs.

Busy Bees

Plants are rooted in one place and cannot move around to meet each other the way animals can. Instead, plants have to rely on messengers to carry their genes. Flowers not only produce male and female cells but also attract the messengers that transport the male cells.

Insects are the messengers employed by many plants to **pollinate** their flowers. On a warm day, millions of insects are busy carrying pollen from flower to flower. Bees, wasps, beetles, flies, and butterflies are effective pollinators — but they each prefer certain types of flowers.

Flowers reward pollinating insects with a sweet liquid food called nectar. Honeybees use it to make honey that they store in wax combs. Other insects drink nectar as an energy-giving food.

But insects do not visit flowers just for the nectar. Pollen itself is a food, rich in protein. Some flowers produce lots of it to attract pollen-eating insects. Such flowers may have no nectar at all.

Left: Woody night-shade flowers only release pollen if they are vibrated. Bumblebees have learned to buzz their wings to obtain the pollen.

Above: Migrant hoverflies wrestle among a forest of stamens in a poppy flower. They eat the pollen grains hungrily.

Right: A snout fly extends its long tongue to sip nectar from a wood cranesbill. Flies pollinate flowers just as effectively as bees.

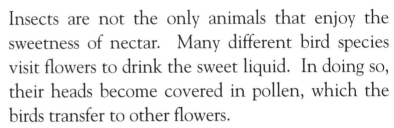

Honey Hunters

Honey Hunters

Top: The beautifully shaped flower of crimson columbine faces downward to keep out rain. Hummingbirds reach the nectar at the tips of the upward-pointing spurs by hovering beneath the flower.

Insects are not the only animals that enjoy the sweetness of nectar. Many different bird species visit flowers to drink the sweet liquid. In doing so, their heads become covered in pollen, which the birds transfer to other flowers.

Many plants produce flowers that are especially designed for bird pollination. Such flowers often hold large pools of nectar to feed these large messengers. If a flower produced only enough nectar to satisfy a bee, then a bird might not bother to visit it. So flowers provide a fitting reward for their own particular messengers.

The hummingbirds of the Americas and the sunbirds of Africa are small, brightly colored birds that feed almost entirely on nectar in the wild. They flit from flower to flower, using this rich energy source to power their rapidly beating wings.

Some mammals also feed on nectar. In Australia, for example, mouse-like animals called honey possums creep among the banksia flowers, lapping nectar and pollinating flowers as they go.

Left: Showy banksia is in flower all year round, providing food for birds and honey possums, such as this one.

One species of vine in Madagascar produces flowers that can only be pollinated by lemurs (relatives of monkeys).

At night among the big trees of many tropical areas, nectar-eating bats feed on the sweet liquid. In turn, they pollinate the heavily scented flowers specially designed to attract them.

Above: A male bronzy sunbird sips nectar from an aloe flower. The bird transfers pollen from its beak and feathers to other aloe flowers.

Borne Away

Left: The female flower of European larch opens to receive wind-borne pollen.

Opposite: The pollen of foxtail barley sheds into the wind.

Messengers that carry pollen from one flower to another need not be winged, or even alive. The wind is also an important carrier of pollen for plants. Just about all of the many kinds of grasses are pollinated by wind. Their pollen is so fine that the grains hang in the air and may be whirled along for hundreds of miles (kilometers) — even into cities, where city dwellers may develop hay fever from breathing pollen-laden air.

Wind pollination is very wasteful because there is no control over where the pollen blows. For this reason, wind-pollinated flowers produce huge quantities of pollen. Perhaps fewer than one grain in a million ever settles on the stigma of the right kind of flower. Many trees, especially pines and other firs, rely on wind as the messenger to carry their pollen. In early summer, these trees can sometimes appear to "smoke," as if they are on fire, when a puff of wind dislodges clouds of pollen from their pale yellow male flowers.

Flowers that are pollinated by the wind do not need to attract messengers, so they have no petals or nectar. They may not even look like "flowers."

Left: A baby spider eats birch pollen caught in its web.

Above: The female flowers of the Engelmann spruce open to receive wind-borne pollen.

17

Smart Flowers

Top: The bee look-alike flowers of the bee orchid may have been originally pollinated by male bumblebees long ago.

Above: This bee-fly has been touched on the back by the stamens and stigma of a triggerplant.

Right: An elbow orchid flower looks like a female wasp. When a male wasp tries to fly off with this "female," a hinge swings him against the orchid's stamens so that pollinia stick to his back.

Plants are not intelligent the way some animals are. They are not able to think or figure things out for themselves. Through millions of years of **evolution**, however, plants have developed some truly amazing ways of fooling insects into working for them. For instance, many orchid flowers look as though they contain nectar, and bees visit them in the hope of obtaining some. Instead, the bee gets two club-shaped blobs of pollen, called **pollinia**, stuck to the top of its head. Within a few minutes, the pollinia bend and hang down over the bee's face. When the bee visits another orchid flower, the pollinia are in just the right position to rub off onto the flower's stigma.

Other orchid flowers are even more cunning. They pretend to be females of certain species of insects — copying an insect's shape, size, color, and scent. When a male insect spots one of these flowers, he is completely fooled and tries to mate with the flower, but what he gets is a crop of pollinia stuck to his back. Fortunately for the orchid, insects do not easily learn to distinguish between a real female and the flower imitation. The male flies off to try to mate with yet another flower, but only succeeds in pollinating it.

Above: A honeybee, visiting a marsh helleborine flower, receives a pair of pollinia that stick to his face. The pollinia are accurately positioned on the bee so that they will rub off on the stigma of the next helleborine flower the bee visits.

Other flowers, such as carrion and wild arum, lure insects with smells. People do not find these smells pleasing because the odor is similar to that of rotten flesh or cow dung. Insects that regularly breed near such unsavory odors are drawn to the flowers. They may even be trapped inside them.

Flowers of the wild arum are pollinated by little, furry insects called owl midges that normally lay their eggs in cow dung. The club-shaped **spadix** in the middle of the wild arum flower produces an odor that smells like dung. It even heats up to help disperse the smell into the air. Midges come from all directions and dive into a hollow around the base of the flower. They cannot escape because the walls are slippery. As many as four thousand midges can be trapped inside a single flower.

Above: Some carrion flowers not only smell bad to humans, but they look bad, too. This species has spheres of black flowers on top of cactus-like stems. Flies are attracted to them.

Right: A fly visits another type of carrion flower in the dry African bush.

Left: The spadix of a wild arum is warm and smelly. Beneath it are whiskers that help trap owl midges in the base of the flower. Below the whiskers are red stamens. Further below are the pale female florets. This flower has been cut open to show the various parts.

Above: An owl midge on the stamens of wild arum is covered with pollen grains.

When the flower first opens, the female florets at its base are ready to receive pollen carried from another flower by midges. A day later, the female florets die and can no longer receive pollen. The male florets then open and produce pollen. The flower begins to shrivel, allowing the midges to escape, covered with new pollen to take to another flower. This clever timing, which enables the female florets to open a day before the male florets, prevents self-fertilization.

The tallest flower in the world is a kind of arum with an 8-foot (2.5-meter)- tall spadix. Tiny bees pollinate it.

Flowers Make Seeds

Top: The yellow-stamened flowers of illyarie produce nuts.

Plants have flowers so that seed production can take place. Seeds are spread far and wide to grow into new plants.

Seed production begins in the ovary. Surrounding the ovary are the beginnings of a kind of box made up of sections called **carpels**. After fertilization, the seeds start to swell. The carpels grow and toughen, forming a seed **pod**.

Of course, not all seeds are contained in pods. In some plants, the carpels form nuts and fruits that animals eat. This is another example of animals doing work for plants and being rewarded for it. They receive food in exchange for spreading the seeds in their droppings.

Right: Poppy flowers produce lidded cups full of small, round seeds. Wind sways the pods, spilling the seeds in all directions.

Left: A yellow-necked mouse makes off with a rose hip. It will eat the hip but discard the seeds, which will grow into new rose bushes.

Seeds themselves contain a rich source of food to help the young plant grow. Often, this food contains a large amount of oil. The corn oil, coconut oil, and palm oil used in cooking are all extracted from the seeds of plants.

Plants require energy to produce seeds. Some plants put all their energy resources into flowering and seeding. They grow for one year, flower and seed, and then die. These plants are called **annuals. Biennials** grow for two years before flowering and then dying. **Perennials** can live for many years. Trees are perennial, and although many trees flower every year, they may have the energy to produce seeds only occasionally.

Above: The pods of rosebay contain many tiny seeds, each surrounded by fine threads to catch the wind.

Left: Each female floret of a wild arum produces a red berry containing a seed. Seeds form only if the florets were fertilized with pollen carried by owl midges from another wild arum.

23

Flower Power

Top: A bitterroot flower bursts forth from the stony ground and opens to face the Sun.

Flowers do not just sit there looking pretty — they are much more active than you might think. Some contain tight "springs," which snap the stamens into action if the flower is touched by an insect. The lower stamens of a plant called broom are contained within two petals of the flower, where they are protected from the Sun and rain. A broom flower that is ready to be pollinated is like a miniature spring trap. The instant a bumblebee touches the flower, the lower stamens snap upward, dusting the underside of the bee with pollen. Broom flowers do not contain nectar. Bumblebees visit them to collect the nutritious pollen that they mix with nectar from other flowers to make a rich paste to feed their young.

Right: The curling lower stamens of broom can be seen in flowers that have been visited by bumblebees. Flowers that have not yet been visited have lower petals clamped shut, holding in the springy stamens.

Above: Red water lilies open wide in the morning Sun.

Above: Before dark, the same red water lilies close tightly.

Other flowers open and close many times during their short lives. They may open on sunny mornings when bees are active and then close at midday or when there is a threat of rain. Many flowers remain tightly closed at night. Bees learn the "opening times" of flowers and often arrive early to be first in line for nectar.

Some flowers, particularly those that grow in cool climates, are able to twist their stalks to face the Sun. They bend and twist to follow the Sun as it moves across the sky. In this way, they collect warmth for visiting insects and to speed the development of seeds.

The Attraction of Flowers

Top: The petals of this blue wood anemone are easily seen by bees.

Above: The oddly shaped bright red flowers of sturt pea attract birds.

Right: This female bronzy sunbird in Africa has a good eye for red flowers. It feeds on a eucalyptus tree.

Many flowers are designed to attract pollinators. Their colors stand out against the green of leaves, so that insects and birds can see them from a distance. Bees are more sensitive to blue, white, and yellow than they are to red. For this reason, there are few native red flowers in Europe, where bees do most of the pollination. In other parts of the world where there are many kinds of red flowers, birds are the main pollinators. Birds see red very well.

It would seem to be a disadvantage for bees and other insects to be blind to red, but they make up for it in another way. They can see **ultraviolet** light. Many flowers have special ultraviolet patterns on their petals, called honey guides, that direct insects to the nectar.

Insects are also very sensitive to smells, and many flowers that insects pollinate are scented. Some flower scents are, to humans, delightful perfumes. Bees seem to share our delight in these scents and are attracted to them. Bird-pollinated flowers usually have little scent because birds rely on sight to find flowers.

Beautiful flowers are true wonders of nature. Their vibrant colors and often enticing scents are a powerful reminder of the intricate relationships flowers have with animals and with the rest of the natural world.

Activities:

Flower Study

Wildflowers are easy to find almost anywhere in the countryside during spring and summer. Even in cities, plants pop up and flower in surprising places, not just in parks and gardens. Old, cracked walls and abandoned yards often provide growing space for a number of different species of flowering plants.

Identification is the first step in any study of flowers. To identify the most flowers possible near you, you will need an illustrated guide covering the plants that grow in your area. You will also need a notebook in which to write down the names of the plants you find. Choose an area, such as a portion of a field or a quiet corner of a park or a city block and see how many flowers you can identify and list.

Compare your plant list with lists of plants that you or your friends find in other areas. Some plants are very choosy about the soil in which they grow. For instance, the species list for clay or chalky areas is very different from the list for sandy areas.

Count the petals of each kind of flower that you identify. Write down whether it has 3, 4, 5, 6, or more petals. Also record the color of the flowers. This will give you an idea of what the likely pollinators are.

Dissecting Flowers

A project for a rainy day involves the study of the inside workings of a flower. You will need a large flower, such as a tulip, daffodil, or lily. Do not pick wildflowers unless you are certain that the species you are taking is very common. Always ask permission of the owner of the land.

A good way to learn the parts of a flower is to make a drawing with colored pencils and label the various parts.

Look closely at the flower and count the number of petals, stamens, and stigmas it contains. Check to see if there are any sepals beneath the petals.

Finally, cut the flower in half longways (*above*) so that each half contains half the stalk as well. You should now be able to see inside the ovary where the seeds are starting to form. If the flower makes nectar, you should also be able to see where the nectar is stored.

Fooling the Bees

Bees are attracted to flowers and quickly learn where to find nectar. But they can easily be attracted to imitation flowers. It is fascinating to watch them learn which imitation flowers are worth visiting.

For this experiment, you will need several sheets of colored paper (various colors), a pencil, scissors, and several bottletops. Draw an outline of a typical flower on one of the sheets of paper and cut it out (*see the paper flowers — above, right*).

Now trace the imitation flower several times on the same colored sheet and on the other colored sheets. Cut out these flowers. You should end up with a collection of paper flowers that are all exactly the same shape but in various colors.

Place your paper flowers on a tabletop outside in a place, such as a garden, where there are honeybees visiting flowers. Weigh down each paper flower with a bottletop at its center. Put a few drops of water in all the bottletops except those that are on, say, the blue flowers. For the blue flowers, put a few drops of a sweet solution — made by mixing sugar or honey in a tablespoonful of warm water — into the bottletops. Now you must wait.

Before long, a bee will discover the sweetened water in the blue flowers. Having had its fill, the bee will fly off to the hive where it will tell other bees — by performing a special dance — where there is a new source of "nectar." Soon, several bees will be buzzing around your imitation flowers and will go to the blue flowers to feed (*below*). Be sure not to harm them.

Move the flowers around from time to time so that the bees do not always find food in the same places.

Next, remove the bottletops containing sweetened water from the blue flowers. Replace them with bottletops containing plain water, and move the flowers around again. Note carefully where the bees land. They should continue to land on the blue flowers even though there is now no reward for them.

This experiment proves that bees can see colors and that they use their eyes and not just their sense of smell to find flowers. It also shows that bees are able to learn quickly and that one bee can tell others where there is a good source of food.

Glossary

annual: a plant that lives for just one year.

biennial: a plant that grows in its first year, flowers in its second year, and then dies.

carpels: parts of a plant, often fleshy, that surround the seeds.

catkin: a tightly packed flower, without petals, produced by many trees. Catkins are either male or female.

cell: the microscopic building block of plant and animal bodies.

dioecious: the condition of having male and female flowers on separate plants.

evolution: a gradual, orderly change from one form to another. Over millions of years, plants and animals evolve into new species.

fertilization: the joining of a male cell with a female cell. Self-fertilization is the fertilization of female cells in a flower by the flower's own male cells (pollen).

floret: a small flower forming part of a group of similar flowers.

genes: the very complex molecules that determine what characteristics are passed on from one generation to the next. There are thousands of genes in a cell. Every cell in a plant or animal contains the same set of genes.

monoecious: the condition of having flowers of both sexes on the same plant.

nectar: sugary liquid produced by flowers to attract insects and other animals.

ovary: the part of a flower or animal that contains the female cells.

perennial: a plant that usually lives for more than two years.

petal: the part of a flower that is normally brightly colored and is intended to attract pollinators.

pod: a box-like structure formed of carpels that contains seeds.

pollen: male cells produced by flowers in the form of fine grains, usually yellow in color. Pollen grains fertilize the female parts of the flowers.

pollinate (pollination): to fertilize with pollen.

pollinia: pollen grains stuck together in blobs, produced mainly by orchids.

sepal: the usually tough outer part of a plant that contains a flower in bud before it opens.

spadix: a club-shape growth in the center of some flowers.

species: animals or plants that are closely related and often similar in behavior and appearance. Members of the same species are capable of breeding together.

stamen: the structure in a flower that produces pollen.

stigma: the structure in a flower that collects pollen so that fertilization can take place.

style: the stalk supporting the stigma.

ultraviolet: radiation that has a wavelength shorter than that of violet light. Ultraviolet light is invisible to humans.

Plants and Animals

The common names of plants and animals vary from language to language. But plants and animals also have scientific names, based on Greek or Latin words, that are the same the world over. Each plant and animal has two scientific names. The first name is called the genus. It starts with a capital letter. The second name is the species name. It starts with a small letter.

aloe (*Aloe secundiflora*) — Africa 15

bronzy sunbird (*Nectarinia kilimensis*) — Africa 15, 26

broom (*Cytisus scoparius*) — Europe 24

creeping thistle (*Cirsium arvense*) — Europe 4-5

dandelion (*Taraxacum species*) — Europe, North America 11

elbow orchid (*Spiculea ciliata*) — Western Australia 18

Engelmann spruce (*Picea engelmannii*) — western North America 17

foxtail barley (*Hordeum jubatum*) — western North America 16-17

goat willow (*Salix caprea*) — Europe, northern Asia, North America 10-11

greater birdsfoot trefoil (*Lotus uliginosus*) — Europe 4-5

hemlock water dropwort (*Oenanthe crocata*) — western Europe 12

honey possum (*Tarsipes spencerae*) — Australia 14

kingcup (*Caltha palustris*) — Europe 27

marjoram (*Origanum vulgare*) — Europe 27

marsh helleborine (*Epipactis palustris*) — Europe 19

morning glory (*Ipomoea leari*) — tropical America, cultivated elsewhere 7

ox-eye daisy (*Leucanthemum vulgare*) — Europe, Asia 7

red campion (*Silene dioica*) — Europe 6

rosebay willowherb (*Epilobium angustifolium*) — Europe, North America 9, 23

showy banksia (*Banksia speciosa*) — Western Australia 14

showy sunray daisy (*Helipterum splendidum*) — Western Australia 5

snout fly (*Rhingia campestris*) — Europe 13

trillium (*Trillium ovatum*) — western North America 6

Books to Read

African Orchids in the Wild and in Cultivation. Isobyl LaCroix (Timber Press)

Flowers, Butterflies and Insects. Sally Morgan (Dover)

The History and Folklore of North American Wildflowers. Tim Coffey (Facts on File)

The Naturalist's Garden: How to Garden with Plants That Attract Birds, Butterflies, and Other Wildlife. Ruth Shaw Ernst (Globe Pequot Press)

Nature Close-ups (series). Densey Clyne (Gareth Stevens)

Videos and Web Sites

Videos

Annuals. (RMI Media)

Flowers, Plants, and Trees. (Library Video)

Gardening from the Ground Up.
   (One Up Productions)

Gardens of the World. (Critics Choice)

Season of Splendor in the Perennial
   Garden. (Creative Images)

Web Sites

www.wild-flowers.com/

www.ars.org/

www.bhglive.com/gardening/index.html

www.mirror.org/groups/ors/index.html

sunsite.sut.ac.jp/multimed/pics/flowers/

homearts.com/depts/garden/12proff1.htm

mail.coos.or.us/~bishop/

Some web sites stay current longer than others. For further web sites, use your search engines to locate the following topics: *flowers, genes, perennials, plants, pollination,* and *seeds.*

Index